ARISE
WITH
SINGING

CHRISTIAN BOSSE

Scripture quotations referenced ESV have been taken from The ESV®
Bible (The Holy Bible, English Standard Version®), copyright © 2001
by Crossway, a publishing ministry of Good News Publishers. Used by
permission. All rights reserved.

Scripture quotations referenced KJV are from the *King James Version* of
the Bible.

Scripture quotations referenced from the New King James Version®.
Copyright © 1982 by Thomas Nelson. Used by permission. All rights
reserved.

Scripture quotations referenced NIV are taken from the Holy Bible, New
International Version®, NIV®. Copyright © 1973, 1978, 1984, 2011 by
Biblica, Inc.™ Used by permission of Zondervan. All rights reserved
worldwide. www.zondervan.com The "NIV" and "New International
Version" are trademarks registered in the United States Patent and
Trademark Office by Biblica, Inc.™

Scripture quotations referenced HCSB®, are taken from the Holman
Christian Standard Bible®, Copyright © 1999, 2000, 2002, 2003, 2009
by Holman Bible Publishers. Used by permission. HCSB® is a federally
registered trademark of Holman Bible Publishers.

Scripture quotations referenced NLT are from the *Holy Bible,* New Living
Translation, copyright © 1996. Used by permission of Tyndale House
Publishers, Inc., Wheaton, Illinois 60189. All rights reserved.

Scripture quotations referenced NASB are from New American Standard
Bible® (NASB), Copyright © 1960, 1962, 1963, 1968, 1971, 1972,
1973, 1975, 1977, 1995 by The Lockman Foundation Used by
permission. www.Lockman.org"

All emphases in Scripture quotations have been added by the author.

ISBN: 1720848165
ISBN-13: 978-1720848165

Thank You, Lord, for giving me wisdom when I was unwise, peace when I was scattered, and joy when I was downtrodden.
To those who have struggled to hear God singing over you, this book is dedicated to you.

Table of Contents

Introduction

We all desire to have a deeper understanding of God and to allow Him to invade our day to day lives. It is an innate desire planted in us from the day of creation. However, we struggle with making this desire a reality. We let life dictate our steps instead of following the ones God ordained. We let people and situations control our emotions. We get lost in a mess of ideas and dreams stemming from decisions we have made in the flesh instead of the Holy Spirit. We easily miss the mark. So, how do we find completion in

Christ when we are living out of our own brokenness?

The answer isn't in the Christian to-do lists we make or the number of volunteer hours we accumulate. We can't pray our way through it. We can't achieve the Christian lifestyle we seek simply by memorizing scripture day in and day out. We can't do anything without Christ. More specifically, we can't grow into the Christians we want to be – and are designed to be – through our own ideas and plans, but only through the power of God.

Though I grew up in a Bible-believing household, it took years for God to convince me of this truth. My life was rarely void of internal conflict, which often opened the door to external chaos. I went through years of making the wrong choices and choosing the wrong relationships. My mind was set on a course for ruin. I was not reflecting Christ in my everyday life.

When I had heard God's voice calling me to Him, I thought I had finally started to understand how life worked. I sought righteousness and strove for perfection. Though I had known better, I believed sin could only be canceled by creating my own sanctification. But I ended up pursuing the Lord with the same thoughts and ideas as the old me. I wasn't a new creation doing new things and enjoying a new life. I was manipulating my faith just like I had manipulated my past. What I didn't know is that the Lord had me on a journey. He was unraveling my self-confidence and destroying my need for perfection. What takes its place is a beautiful song of confidence in the Lord.

The inspiration for this book came slowly. Like little whispers throughout the years, God has urged me to write about the wisdom He has imparted to me. He yearns for His children to gain power through the captivating nature of the

Holy Spirit and the heartsong He has placed in each of us. The Lord was meticulous to take His sweet time cultivating the orchestra of salvation, redemption, and sanctification to allow us to experience pure worship with Him.

This book is not an in-depth, step-by-step guide on how to grow in Christ. It won't give you a list of things to do to see God move in your life. It doesn't come with any of those promises. Why? Because your walk with Christ is an exchange. How you choose to invest your heart into this journey is equal to what results you will get out of it. You must connect with the instruction, encouragement, and revelation each chapter holds. You must set out to see real transformation in your life to truly experience it. Once you make that decision, you will be able to discover God's intentions for you as you read this book.

Trust me, it isn't going to be easy. God is pruning you, and that means there are some traits and behaviors He will need to cut down to the stem. He is pulling you away from the comfortability of the imaginable and is placing you in the midst of mystery. It is not to harm you or confuse you. It is for your good and the good of the Kingdom.

So, please take your time as you marinate in each chapter of this book. Re-read this book as needed. Allow yourself to run into the twists and turns of life. Let the Lord dictate your steps. He will guide you in the right direction. You only need to follow His lead. Don't pull your hand from His. Don't step away because it isn't easy and doesn't make sense. Let it shake you out of the status quo so that you arise from each moment, each season, and each storm of life singing the song within you. He put it there to be heard. So, let it be heard. May you find your voice and let it be known, without hesitation. May you be transformed by His power and His light. It all starts with the decision to truly engage with God as you read this book. Will you? Your transformation starts now.

GOD CREATED EACH
OF US WITH THE
LONGING TO PRAISE.
SO, WHY ARE WE
SILENT?

CHRISTIAN BOSSE

Chapter One

There is a Sound

What does it mean to worship God with your whole heart? Man has asked this question millennial after millennial. After all this time, we've barely scratched the surface.

Worship may have been reduced to the musical experience between man and who/what he serves, but it was never intended that way. From the beginning of time, God has desired His children to dwell in a state of worship. He wishes for us to melt into the depths of what it means to worship with our entire lives.

When Adam and Eve chose to be like God out of their own strength, the original concept of worship became a distant memory. Our wisdom on the topic was stolen away. The deceit of the devil led us down a path of confusion, barring us from experiencing worship in its purest form. The Fall placed us on a trajectory where we floated aimlessly in the opposite direction than the one we were created for. We began engaging in a man-made, imperfect form of worship. Worship turned into a limited and fractured portion. No longer could we encounter God His way. No, we found ourselves scattered, seeking to worship anything and everything instead of Him. Through our newfound knowledge of good *and* evil, we learned to replace our perfect God with imperfect people and things.

But God has worked feverishly to fix this broken system. He has worked to bring us back to Him so we can experience pure and total worship. God has been chasing us down from the moment we wandered off. He sent His Son to break us out of our captivity. He knows we cannot experience the fullness of life, both here on Earth and in Heaven, without His perfect and complete presence.

There is a day we will meet the Father in the sky and enter the worship we were created for. We will feast our eyes and hearts, filling up on what we lost. We will join with the four living creatures surrounding the throne, eternally praising "holy, holy, holy is the Lord God Almighty, who was and is and is to come" (Revelation 4:8).

While we ourselves can never create a worship experience like this, we can seek God in hopes of getting a glimpse of true worship. We can get a taste of pure worship encounter here on Earth by seeking the Lord above all else.

You were created with a sound. The Word of God – that is the Bible – says that God said, "Let Us make mankind in our image," and so we were created (Genesis 1:26). God breathed into man's nostrils the breath of life and we lived (Genesis 2:7). It was this sound God made that spoke purpose into our lives. You were designed to produce a sound, as well.

Regardless of what you do in life, your life is producing a sound. The way you live is singing a song. It may or may not be the song you were intended to sing. God wrote a song unique to your story for you to sing. When you choose to live life your way, replacing the perfect God with other people and things, you choose to sing an imperfect song. You choose to sing a song you put together at a moment's notice.

On the contrary, if you belong to the Lord, you want to sing the song written for you. Your soul desperately craves to be made complete through the purest form of worship. Despite this innate desire, you must submit to the will of God before you can dive into this adventure.

Let me put it this way, you are a house made of cards. Alone, you are temporary. God comes along and topples you over. He rids you of all human desires and self-confidence in the undoing. Meanwhile, He works with you, rebuilding you on the Cornerstone – His transfigured Word. He makes you stronger. You are no longer a flimsy house of cards. You are mighty because He is mighty. You are becoming a house of bricks, no longer temporary but eternal.

However, when you choose to stop the process, you choose to be an incomplete shell of the Lord's design. You choose to only be a frame of the complete work. Jesus walks by with the Holy Spirit beside Him, and they talk about how they wish more could be done. But you're allowing sin, flesh, and fear to determine the sound you make. You are clinging on to the unfinished, mortal being instead of reaching for the consummated eternal life you were created for.

God longs to redirect your heart so that you can tune in to His melody. The undoing may be a process of change over a lifetime, but it is only the beginning of where He wants to take you. Don't close your eyes. Don't clench your fists in fear. Surrender your heart to the unwinding of your self-reliance. Embark on this journey so you can arise singing the song of the Lord.

Chapter Two

In the Presence

Worship happens in the dwelling place. It happens in the place and time set apart for the sole purpose of meeting with God.

The presence of God isn't a natural place in the physical realm. While God does often appear in natural places and specified times, He appears in the supernatural, giving us an awareness of His incomprehensible presence.

The presence of God is atmospheric. Like the pillar of cloud in Exodus, God's glory settles upon us transporting our spirits from the natural to the supernatural.

But The Fall divided us from God, hindering our ability to draw near to Him. The natural world competes with the supernatural, causing us to engage in spiritual warfare.

Most of our spiritual battles are fought in our minds. We wrestle with the lies of the enemy. We fight against self-depreciating thoughts. We combat negative emotions that lure us to sin. Our sin, the flesh, and worldly influences interfere with our time with God. These roadblocks distract us from having a real encounter, causing us to be stagnant in our relationship with God. We find ourselves singing songs of bitterness, judgment, pride, and lust instead of songs of grace, joy, peace, and purity. Our hearts become calloused and we turn to idol worship.

To counteract the division between you and God, you must first seek regular time in His presence. There is no song to sing if you aren't regularly meeting with the composer. The presence of the Lord is like an all-you-can-eat buffet. God longs for you to come and eat. Fill up your plate until your food spills over the sides. Eat until you can't even breathe, and when you have room, eat again!

Next, you must also remove all barriers and distractions. If God intends for us to abide in Him, and He in us, then you can be assured it is the devil's intention to keep us divided. He wants to deceive us, causing us to experience a limited encounter with God.

One of the devil's tactics is to blind our spiritual eyes using distractions. For many, this looks like having a tough time logging off social media to pray. Or, you might often find yourself choosing entertainment over prayer time. If you have a tough time settling into the presence of God, you are being led astray. Remember, you are fighting a spiritual battle in your mind. Don't give in to distractions. Command your mind to focus. Seek the Lord with an uncontainable desperation. If you must get away from everything and everyone to give Him your undivided attention, do it. Your spiritual well-being is worth any sacrifice you can give.

Lastly, go to God ready to listen. Coming to God humbly and wholeheartedly allows for unlimited access. The Bible says in Ecclesiastes 5:2,

> "do not be quick with your mouth,
> Do not be hasty in your heart
> To utter anything before God."

Allow God to speak to you. This is the primary reason for meeting with Him. The Old Testament is full of encounters between God and man.

Every time, God speaks directly to man, often saying more than the person He is talking to.

Stop narrating your problems to God. He is fully aware of the troubles you face. He understands that you need a breakthrough. The Lord draws you near, so you can hear Him clearly. However, you can't have a conversation if you're the only one talking. Be quiet. Make the dwelling place holy ground by submitting to the authority of the Holy God.

This is the foundation of living a life of worship. It starts with open communication with God. Intentionally set aside time with Him. Do away with distractions. Choose to listen, instead of making it all about you. Have community with God, bridging the gap between the natural and the supernatural.

Chapter Three

Know the Lyrics

Jesus came so that we could have abundant lives, but He never promised that we would be trouble-free. Whether big or small, we all have storms that threaten to strip us of our peace.

James encourages us in his letter to "consider it pure joy… whenever [we] face trials of many kinds, because [we] know that the testing of [our] faith produces perseverance' (James 1:2-3). Yet, many of us find ourselves weak and weary amid trials. Why?

Though God has already won the victory, we choose to believe that we are losing the fight. We don't pick up our weapons to fight our battles. Our swords are left at home. We enter spiritual warfare in hopelessness or pride because we believe we must fight in our own strength.

In Ephesians 6:10-13, it says,

"be strong in the Lord and His mighty power. Put on the full armor of God so that you can take your stand against the devil's schemes. For our struggle is not against flesh and blood, but against the rulers, against the authorities, against the powers of this dark world and against the spiritual forces of evil in the heavenly realms. Therefore, put on the full armor of God, so that when the day of evil comes, you may be able to stand your ground, and after you have done everything, to stand."

Christ rose, raising us up alongside Him. We are not insignificant bystanders. We are warriors in His heavenly army. Even so, we let the negative voices and influences cause us to run around scattered instead of standing firm.

A little later in the same chapter of Ephesians, we are commanded to take up "the sword of the Spirit, which is the word of God" (Ephesians 6:17). But we are barely flipping a page in our Bibles. We aren't fighting our battles through scripture, prayer, and praise. We are settling for defeat with our defenses down.

Do we really know scripture? Or do we stop at being able to quote the quintessential Christian verses? Even then, how many of us can say we know the exact book, chapter, and verse those well-known verses come from?

It is sad how biblically illiterate we are. We allow our pastors to do our job of studying scripture. We expect them to read the Bible for us and relay the information in a perfect message that makes sense to each of us individually. Frustration and disappointment flood our hearts when the scripture isn't read in our favorite translation or when the message doesn't fit our present situation. We're lazy, high-maintenance, spoiled Christians. We'd rather sit back and get spoon-fed the word once a week than open an app on our phone or flip a page in our paper Bibles.

The Word of God is a massive archive of spiritual lyrics. These lyrics are to be memorized, meditated on, and shouted over your life. In Deuteronomy 11:18-19 we are instructed to fix the Word of God

"in [our] hearts and minds; tie them as symbols on [our] hands and bind them on [our] foreheads. Teach them to [our] children, talking about them when [we] sit at home and when [we] walk along the road, when [we] lie down and when [we] get up."

How can we possibly sing the melody of life God has written for the each of us if we are busy singing the wrong words?

You might be singing "I have no purpose in life" instead of "'For I know the plans I have for you,' declares the Lord, 'plans to prosper you and not to harm you, plans to give you a hope and a future" (Jeremiah 29:11). You might be hearing the deafening tones of fear and stress when you should hear the beauty of "be anxious for nothing, but in everything by prayer and supplication, with thanksgiving let your requests be made known to God" (Philippians 4:6).

Real transformation comes when we study scripture in its context and listen to God's instruction. It happens when we memorize Bible verses, speaking them over our lives *daily*.

As a result, your mind will begin to change. You will develop the fruit of the Spirit, enabling you to be more loving, kind, at peace, and full of self-control. Storms won't shake you down to the core. You will be able to put into practice the Word of God, declaring the Bible over trials and tribulations. Faith will rise within you, not because you see immediate results, but because you trust in God's promises and believe that He is always faithful.

If you're living life with a head-knowledge of the Word of God, but not a heart-knowledge of it, you're truly missing the point of Christianity. Jesus came to give us life more abundantly (John 10:10), so why are you living a life of less than? Don't sing whatever words come to mind. Use the power God gave you. Use the Bible to experience the abundant life He has set before you. Memorize the right lyrics so you can be strengthened and encouraged.

Chapter Four

Open Your Mouth

Now that the foundation has been laid, it is time to learn how to sing. Your God-given song is first vocalized when you declare the Word of God over your life and the lives of others.

Sadly, many of us aren't doing an excellent job of declaring the Word of God. Scripture has become an underrated part of our lives. We write them down in our journals. Bible verses are hung in our bedrooms, offices, and living rooms. We quote them when we're encouraging others. We use scripture to call people out on their sins and mistakes. Many Christians know and use scripture. But we don't use it *appropriately* and *effectively*.

The Bible, while it is an exquisite story about God's love and sacrifice, was not written for you to feel better about yourself. I'm sure you're scratching your head at that. That is because for decades the Bible has been presented to the world as a love story. But that wasn't God's original intention.

Yes, He loves us so much that He gave the ultimate sacrifice so that we could be brought near to Him. However, the story does not stop at salvation. I'll say it again: *the story does not stop at salvation*. Let me remind you that we serve a resurrected Savior and King, who is seated at the right hand of the Father "*far* above all rule and authority, power and dominion, and every name that is invoked, not only in the present age but also in the one to come" (Ephesians 1:21).

So, why are we living our lives rooted in this world? We run around obsessed with the actions and opinions of others. Our minds are consumed with collecting earthly possessions and living prosperous lives. We wander like lost children in the wilderness, constantly questioning why we are on this Earth, asking God if we are supposed to get this job or live at that place or marry this person. God cares about the direction you take, but He says that none of this really matters!

Again, God's Word was not written for you to feel better. It wasn't inspired so you could get a pat on the back. God didn't appoint dozens of authors to pen His words over thousands of years so that you could feel better about yourself. The Bible was divinely inspired so that you could be made whole and share this power with the entire world. This is not an effortless process. It will challenge you to move beyond your fears and feelings to walk in faith.

One of the most important steps in this journey is the memorization and declaration of scripture. Scripture memorization is for the encouragement and edification of our faith. The Apostle Paul writes in Romans 10 that faith comes by hearing the Word of God. He later says in chapter 12 that transformation comes when we renew our minds. We cannot take this lightly! We must study the Bible like a textbook, letting the instructions guide us to living in the *full* power of the Holy Spirit.

We must not settle for merely knowing scripture. That leads us to live subpar lives. That results in accepting healing and breakthrough without truly accessing it. It is vital we dig deep into the Word, meditating on the truth. Devour scripture, planting it in the depths of your heart. This is how you live a conquered life. This is how you begin to arise with singing.

Get your Bible out. Intentionally study an entire book, piece by piece, over the course of a month, season or year. Take time to read the same verses over and over. Make the Word of God the lyrics in the background of your mind.

Then, when you face the trouble that will inevitably come your way, you won't settle for half of a miracle. You won't settle for a partial breakthrough. Your faith will be strengthened. You will rise up and pray "no weapon formed against me shall prosper, and every tongue that rises against me, You shall condemn" (Isaiah 54:17). When your children are lost, you'll remember that when you trained them in the way of the Lord, His Word promised that "when [they] are old [they] will not depart from it" (Proverb 22:6). When you're tired of the same person always getting on your nerves, you won't desperately wish to have peace in the moment. You'll be able to remind yourself that "Fools vent their anger, but the wise quietly hold it back" (Proverb 29:11).

No, the Bible is not for your comfortability. It is for your boldness. The Bible was written to provide wisdom and spiritual nourishment. Actively engaging in God's Word causes you to move beyond wading through the trenches of trouble and sin.

You are to sing the song of scripture. You are to make praise the fuel of your faith. Your life will no longer be preoccupied with what *could* have been and what *should* have been. You will rise with singing when you read the Word, believe the Word, and do and speak the Word. Don't settle for a life of striving. Believe, and you'll live a life of thriving.

Chapter Five

Rejoice

Life has its ups and downs. Though trials come our way, more often we are tripped up by smaller conflicts.

One bad moment can shift the course of an entire day or week when we let it. Little issues sprout like weeds. Anger, bitterness, and disappointment increases when smaller problems begin to pile up.

Declaring the Word of God isn't only for the larger complications in your life. In fact, most of the battles we face occur in a single day or moment. By limiting the power of God to the biggest battles, we only tap into a portion of our inheritance as children of God.

It is imperative we learn how to sing in the tiny trials. We need to exercise our faith, building up endurance by speaking into the little moments.

Proverbs 17:22 reveals that "a joyful heart is good medicine, but a crushed spirit dries up the bones." A crushed spirit is commonly developed by repetitively speaking doubt and negativity. It is the result of continually believing that the glass is half empty. But, I want you to know that whether the glass is half full, half empty, or bone dry it is full of something! It may only contain air, but at least it is full of it!

Brothers and sisters, "take delight in the Lord, and He will give you the desires of your heart" (Psalm 37:4). Start by speaking verses involving praise. The Bible is full of examples, both in the Old and New Testament. Get some notecards or sticky notes out and write them down. Fill your heart with scriptures that inspire you to rejoice.

Furthermore, look at what is influencing you. Are you consumed with celebrities and reality TV? Are you listening to secular music all day long? What kind of company do you keep? Are they encouraging you when you're down? Or are their mouths continually spewing out complaints, hatred, and negativity?

When the world around you is dark and dim, it is hard to see the light. Make changes to the music you listen to and the TV you watch. Add uplifting influences to your day-to-day activities. Fortify yourself, so you can be firmly planted in the joy of the Lord.

Search for mini miracles unfolding around you. *Smile*. Command your heart to be delighted. It might seem trivial, but those everyday frustrations are weighing you down. They're tricking you into giving in to doubt and negativity. They're sowing itty bitty seeds of contempt, hardening your heart slowly but surely.

In the words of the Apostle Paul,

"fix your thoughts on what is true, and honorable, and right, and pure, and lovely, and admirable. Think about things that are excellent and worth of praise" (Philippians 4:7 NLT).

Surrender your thoughts and emotions to the authority of the Holy Spirit. Rejoice in the little victories. Count every blessing you can find. Start journaling a record of all the things you are thankful for. Praise the Lord for He is good. He is faithful when your life is a mess and when seems put together. You always have something to sing about, so choose to sing songs of joy. Then, gladness will overtake your heart, causing your heart to hum a happy tune no matter the situation or circumstance.

Chapter Six

Center Stage

"What am I called to do? What's next?"

This is one of the most common questions we ask ourselves. We are preoccupied with the task of stepping into the next position in the next season. We are title-driven, striving to be excellent at a specific profession or skillset. We continually ask ourselves and others what they are currently doing and what they want to do with their lives. It starts when we're young. Children are asked at an early age what they would like to be when they grow up. But the question frequently comes with strings attached.

The truth is, our world is so engrossed with position and occupation that we forget God has already designated a position for every one of us. We grasp at the highest paying job or the most prestigious status in our career field. We look for financial security as if our eternal destinies depend on it. All the while, we toil aimlessly, never once fulfilling God's calling for our lives.

Your life is a uniquely written and orchestrated song presenting the Gospel for the glory of the Lord. God loves to see His children prosper, but He isn't so consumed with our prosperity that He overlooks our purpose.

Many of us go through seasons of wandering. Whether or not we follow through with our cookie-cutter plans, we all have times where we feel lost. We desperately hunt for purpose. This is because we live life with a resumé mentality.

We work to produce a list of all the things we have done. On the contrary, the true goal is not to come to the end of our lives and say, "look at what I've done", but "look at how I have lived." This is what happens when we shift from being resumé-driven to being eulogy-focused.

What do you want people to say about you when you die? Would you rather they commend you for the status you achieved at work or the number of possessions you owned? Or do you want them to say you were full of kindness and displayed Christ in all that you did, no matter what the cost?

Don't get me wrong, what you do with your life matters. However, God is far less concerned with the minor details of what you do and is much more concerned with what you do with what He's given you.

We are all given gifts and talents. Some are gifted with the adept ability to draw. Others have a mastery in creating and running business. Some are talented authors and salespeople, while others are impeccable at being generous. We all have at least one gift God has given us. The question is: are you managing yours well?

Take, for example, the Parable of the Talents in Matthew 25:14-30. Jesus is teaching about the Kingdom of Heaven when He tells a story about a man going on a journey. This man entrusts three of his servants with his property while he is gone. He gives each servant a different number of talents, according to the abilities of each servant. When he returns, he calls each of his servants to give an account of what they did with the property he had given to them.

Two of the servants had traded their talents, making more talents than they originally had. Meanwhile, the third servant buried his talent into the ground and dug it back up to give to his master when his master had returned. The first two servants were commended for their faithfulness, while the third was thrown out into the darkness.

Without even scratching the surface of this passage, there is something I think we often miss when reading this parable. Notice, the master gave to each servant the number of talents according to his abilities, but not one servant was given specific instruction as to what to do with the talents they had received. And, yet, two of the servants were still faithful with what they were given. How?

There must have been an understanding that when the master entrusted them with his property, they were to do something that would please the master. Not only did they know they were to please their master. They also knew that wisely investing in what they received *is* what pleases the master.

You might desire to be a doctor, an author, or a plumber. You have the free will to pursue each of these professions. But that doesn't mean you are wisely investing in the gifts and talents God has given you.

Let's say you do end up being a doctor, author, or plumber. You might be one of the best in your field. You are good at what you do, but you have a gift for teaching. If you are not also teaching others in your career as a doctor, author or plumber, you aren't wisely investing in the gifts God gave you. You are simply blending in, hiding your talent in the dirt until the day you die.

Your talents are God-given. No one else can determine your destiny. It has already been written. Stop putting the opinions of yourself and others above God's call over your life. You run this race of life not to impress with your speed or might, but your endurance and faithfulness. Quit running this race fixed on temporary, earthly goals, and start fixing your eyes on the eternal story God has written just for you.

What do you want God to say to you when you die? Would you rather He tell you that your fear of man and your concern with reputation kept you from doing what He called you to do? Or do you want Him to congratulate you on being a faithful servant, using the gifts you have been given to give Him glory?

This is what it means to sing the song you were created for. It means getting up on stage, in front of your friends, family, colleagues and even strangers. It means walking center stage to a single microphone. It looks like opening your mouth, singing *your* song, and no one else's.

Chapter Seven

Serenade Someone

Now, you are falling in sync with your God-given song. The more you practice the lessons you have learned, the easier it is to sing the melody within you.

If you are truly walking in the tune that God composed for you, your song won't be held in secret. It will be difficult to contain it. Music will pour out of you almost effortlessly.

Did you know that your heartsong isn't for your spiritual ears only? It is meant to be shared with someone else.

Our modern sense of community is lacking. In this century, we are more divided mentally and emotionally than we are physically. Hundreds of thousands of people gather in amphitheaters and concert halls for the same purpose of hearing a speaker, rapper, or singer, but many leave knowing the same amount of people they knew when they arrived. We sit in coffee shops, offices, and churches rarely going deeper than a casual "hi, how are you?"

Building relationships is a challenging task if your heart isn't in the right place. It is not uncommon for us to seek belonging and self-worth by entering a new relationship. In fact, many of us desire community due to personal need and desire. Going into a friendship or relationship self-focused results in patchy, uncommitted connections.

Jesus implores us in John 13:34-35 to love each other as He has loved us, and "by this

everyone will know that [we] are [His] disciples."
We can't love one another without understanding
God's love for us. It is a gift we cannot earn and
never will deserve.

Have you ever wondered why God created
us? He is omnipotent, omnipresent, and
omniscient. God has no needs (Acts 17:25). Yet,
He created us, and He did so on purpose.
Furthermore, when we continue to turn our
backs on Him, God gives us the gifts of salvation,
grace, and mercy through His Son, Jesus. He
extends wisdom, guidance, and power through
the Holy Spirit (John 14:26). It is evident that He
loves us dearly.

God doesn't simply give love, He *is* love (1
John 4:8). Therefore, God works in us and
through us to love others around us. We find our
belonging and worth in Him. We don't seek
fulfillment in others, because God is the only one
who can fulfill us.

Spending time in the presence of the Lord, studying His word, and walking in the power of the Holy Spirit nourishes our souls. Our needs are taken care of by God. Loving relationships are created as a byproduct of finding sustenance and fulfillment in Christ. Now we can use our God-given gifts to bless others.

Your presence *is* and should be a gift unto others. Not because you are the gift, but because God within you is a blessing to be shared. You bear *His* image to be a light in the lives of those around you.

Sing your song aloud to others. Share your testimony to inspire someone. Show the people around you that they, too have something to sing about. Teach others the lessons you have learned, reminding them of their freedom in Christ. Grow relationships in love and not brokenness. Serenade your friends and loved ones in love.

Chapter Eight

Pass It On

This is the end. And, yet, it is only the beginning.

By now, I hope you have learned how to cultivate a worshipful life. I hope your heart, mind, and soul has been altered by the words in this book.

This last phase is among the most crucial aspects of our faith: bearing witness. Christians and non-believers alike know that this is an essential part of Christianity. However, many of us modern-day Christians have unfavorable opinions regarding the act of witnessing.

No matter what your opinion is, God requires us to bear witness of His light. The Great Commission is a passage in the book of Matthew outlining what Jesus commanded His disciples to do before ascending to Heaven. He implores them to

"go, therefore, and make disciples of all nations, baptizing them in the name of the Father and of the Son and of the Holy Spirit, teaching them to observe everything [He has] commanded [them to do]" (Matthew 28:19-20).

Therefore, we must share the goodness of God, shedding His light on the dark world we live in.

Efficiently bearing witness is a direct result of our spiritual health. Our lack of understanding the power we're given by the Holy Spirit is one of the main reasons we fail to effectively witness to the world. Unfortunately, we make sharing our faith about ourselves, worrying about our reputation, comfortability, and history. We disqualify ourselves based on our flawed, sinful nature.

On the other hand, we also disqualify others from hearing the Word of God because we deem them too far gone. We look at their sins and decide their eternal destiny is sealed forever.

Bearing witness requires us to look at all God has to offer and measure it far above our excuses. If you continually disqualify yourself, you settle for being a bystander instead of a mighty warrior in the King's army. You allow spiritual warfare to overtake others due to your own shortcomings.

The Apostle Paul shares, "it is written: 'I believed; therefore, I have spoken.' Since we have that same spirit of faith, we also believe and therefore speak" (2 Corinthians 4:13). We don't have to be perfect to proclaim the goodness of God. We simply must believe.

Earlier in that same chapter, Paul writes that "we have this treasure in jars of clay to show that this all-surpassing power is from God and not from us" (2 Corinthians 4:7). No matter who you are, you are an imperfect person. Instead of hiding the light within you due to your own flaws and failures, be transparent with others. Show them that following Christ doesn't require perfection, but faith.

And if you're disqualifying others from hearing the Gospel because of their actions, evaluate your life. We are all sinners alike. We are not entitled to God's grace and mercy. It is not our responsibility to judge the world. Pay attention to what Jesus tells us in Luke 6:37-38,

> "do not judge, and you will not be judged. Do not condemn, and you will not be condemned. Forgive, and you will be forgiven. Give, and it will

be given to you. A good measure, pressed down, shaken together and running over, will be poured into your lap. For with the measure you use, it will be measured to you."

Barring others from receiving Jesus is contrary to the inerrant Word of God. If you submit to the wisdom God has given to you in this book, you will quickly come to realize that this is unacceptable in the Kingdom. The Body of Christ is not an exclusive club. We mustn't treat it as such.

Be a catalyst for positive change in the world around you, not by domineering and judging others, but by witnessing Christ. Remind yourself that *everything* you have is from the Lord. Be an image-bearer, reflecting the light of Christ due to a reverence and respect for our Almighty God.

God has given you this one voice. Your song produces a sound unique to you. When you seek the God and His kingdom, you become a vessel of His presence to the world around you.

You were created on purpose for a purpose. Don't pass through life with a passive faith. Activate the heartsong within you. Look to God for wisdom and walk in the boldness of the Holy Spirit. You are a child of the Most High God. May you arise with singing today and forever more.

DEVOUR SCRIPTURE,

PLANTING IT IN

THE DEPTHS OF

YOUR HEART.

CHRISTIAN BOSSE

Scripture References

Chapter One:

- Revelation 4:8 NIV
- Genesis 1:26 NIV
- Genesis 2:7 NIV

Chapter Two:

- Ecclesiastes 5:2 NIV

Chapter Three:

- James 1:2-3 NIV
- Ephesians 6:10-13 NIV
- Ephesians 6:17 NIV
- Deuteronomy 11:18-19 NIV
- Jeremiah 29:11 NIV
- Philippians 4:6 NKJV
- John 10:10 KJV

Chapter Four:

- Ephesians 1:21 NIV
- Romans 10:17 KJV
- Romans 12:2 NASB
- Isaiah 54:17 NKJV
- Proverb 22:6 ESV
- Proverb 29:11 NLT

Chapter Five:

- Proverb 17:22 ESV
- Psalm 37:4 NIV
- Philippians 4:7 NLT

Chapter Six:

- Matthew 25:14-30 ESV

Chapter Seven:

- John 13:34-35 NIV
- Acts 17:25 NLT
- John 14:26 NIV
- 1 John 4:8 ESV

Chapter Eight:

- Matthew 28:19-20 HCSB
- 2 Corinthians 4:13 NIV
- 2 Corinthians 4:7 NIV
- Luke 6:37-38 NIV

PRAYER IS THE MOST IMPORTANT SPIRITUAL WEAPON TO FIGHT YOUR BATTLES. DON'T LEAVE IT BEHIND AT HOME WHEN GOING TO THE BATTLEFIELD.

CHRISTIAN BOSSE

BIBLE VERSES FOR PRAYER AND DECLARATION

Verses for Prayer and Declaration
Joy & Hope

- Isaiah 12:5 ESV
- Proverb 17:22 ESV
- Psalm 63:3 NLT
- 2 Samuel 22:50 HCSB
- 1 Thessalonians 5:16-18 NKJV
- Zephaniah 3:17 NKJV
- Psalm 37:4 NIV
- Philippians 4:4 NKJV
- Psalm 118:24 NKJV
- Hebrews 11:1 NIV
- Psalm 34:19 NKJV
- Lamentations 3:21-22 NLT
- Hebrews 6:19 HCSB
- Proverb 13:12 NIV
- Jeremiah 29:11 NIV
- Psalm 147:11 NIV
- Ephesians 6:16 HCSB
- Proverb 18:10 NIV

Verses for Prayer and Declaration
Boldness & Courage

- Deuteronomy 31:8 HCSB
- Psalm 56:3-4 ESV
- Isaiah 41:10 NLT
- Proverb 28:1 ESV
- Ephesians 6:10-13 NIV
- Psalm 27:1 KJV
- Joshua 1:9 NKJV
- Isaiah 41:13 NIV
- 2 Timothy 1:7 NKJV
- Psalm 27:14 NLT
- Isaiah 54:17 NKJV

Verses for Prayer and Declaration
Peace & Faith

- James 3:18 NIV
- Philippians 4:6 NKJV
- Romans 8:6 NKJV
- Psalm 23:2 ESV
- Isaiah 26:3 NLT
- Matthew 5:9 NIV
- Jeremiah 17:7 HCSB
- Psalm 119:165 NLT
- Numbers 6:26 NKJV
- Psalm 104:14 NKJV
- James 1:19 HCSB
- Isaiah 55:11 NKJV

Verses for Prayer and Declaration
Wisdom & Integrity

- Proverb 21:21 ESV
- Psalm 37:30 NKJV
- Proverb 1:7 NIV
- Ephesians 5:15-16 NLT
- Proverb 29:11 NLT
- John 8:31-32 ESV
- Proverb 17:24 ESV
- James 3:17 NIV
- Proverb 24:5 HCSB
- Esther 4:14 NIV
- Colossians 3:23 ESV
- Proverb 12:27 AMP

Verses for Prayer and Declaration
Healing & Freedom

- Psalm 91:6-7 NLT
- Isaiah 38:16-17 NIV
- Philippians 4:19 NIV
- Isaiah 53:5 NKJV
- 2 Corinthians 3:17 ESV
- Proverb 4:20-22 NLT
- James 5:14-16 NIV
- John 8:36 NLT
- Psalm 119:45 NLT
- 1 Peter 2:16 ESV
- Romans 8:1-2 NIV

Recommended Reads

- *Prayer* by Timothy Keller
- *Streams of Living Water* by Richard Foster
- *In His Image* by Jen Wilkin
- *Driven by Eternity* by John Bevere
- *Discerning the Voice of God* by Priscilla Shrier
- *The Pursuit of God* by A.W. Tozer
- *Prayer* by Richard Foster
- *Victory Over Darkness* by Neil T. Andersen
- *Invitation to a Journey* by M. Robert Mulholland
- *Spiritual Formation* by Henri Nouwen
- *The Believer's Authority* by Kenneth Hagen
- *Worship* by A.W. Tozer
- *The Weight of Glory* by C.S. Lewis

About the Author

Photo taken by Laura Campbell

Creative and driven, Christian Bosse writes inspiring and challenging books and online articles. She has a background in women's ministry, young adult ministry, and nonprofit organizations. Christian is passionate about counseling and biblical literacy. Christian is a Kansas City native, currently residing there with her wonderful husband and beautiful daughter.

GET CONNECTED
Facebook: facebook.com/christianbosseofficial
Instagram and Twitter: @christianbosse_

96171964R00046

Made in the USA
Middletown, DE
29 October 2018